Visit Hal Leonard Online at
www.halleonard.com

Email: ausadmin@halleonard.com.au
Cheltenham, Victoria, 3192 Australia
4 Lentara Court
Hal Leonard Australia Pty. Ltd.
In Australia Contact:

HAL•LEONARD®
CORPORATION
7777 W. BLUEMOUND RD. P.O. Box 13819 MILWAUKEE, WI 53213

ISBN 978-1-4234-6253-8

Clarinet Concerto No. 1 in F Minor, Op. 73

(1786-1826)

WEBER

Carl Maria von

Classical
HAL•LEONARD

PREFACE

The Hal Leonard Classical Play-Along™ series allows you to work through great classical works systematically and at any tempo with accompaniment.

Tracks 2-4 on the CD demonstrate the concert version of each movement. After tuning your instrument to Track 1 you can begin practicing the piece. Using the Amazing Slow-Downer technology included on the CD, you can adjust the recording to any tempo you like without altering the pitch. (Note that when using Amazing Slow-Downer, the CD will stop after each track instead of playing continuously.)

- Track No. ⬚1 – tuning notes
- Track numbers in circles ◯ – concert version
- Track numbers in diamonds ◆ – play-along version

CONCERT VERSION

Gerhard Kraßnitzer, Clarinet

Austrian Symphony Orchestra-Burgenland

Boris Perrenoud, Conductor

CONCERTO No. 1 Op. 73

for Clarinet in F-minor

I ②

C. M. v. Weber (1786 - 1826)

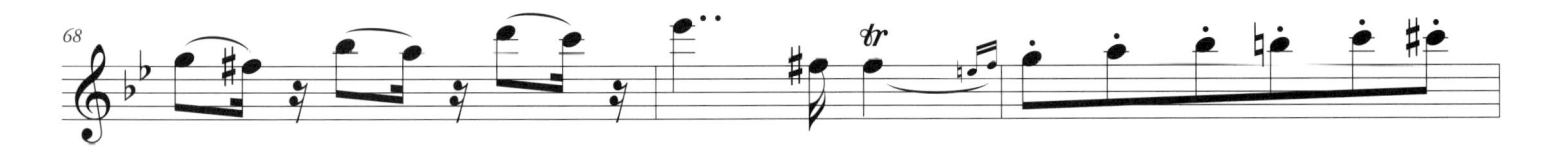

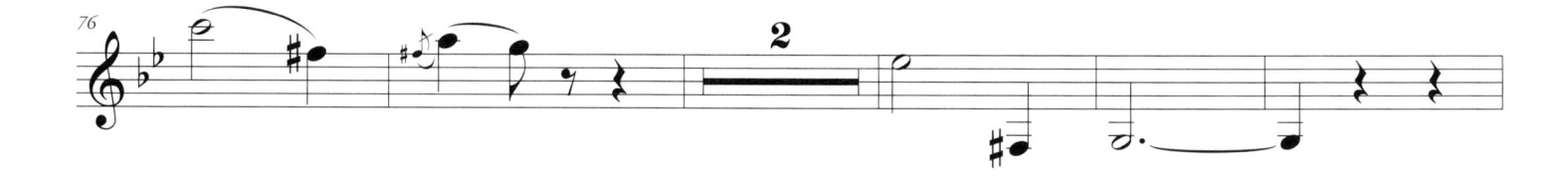

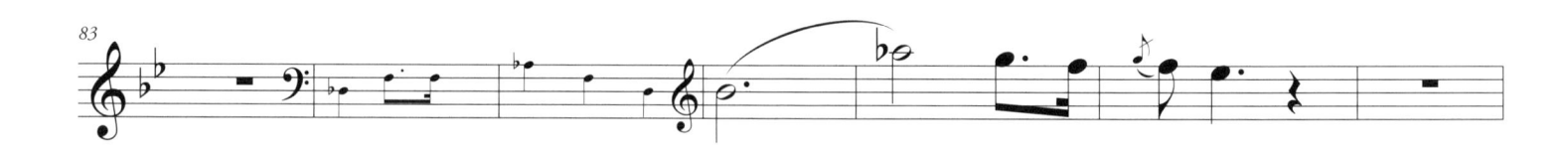

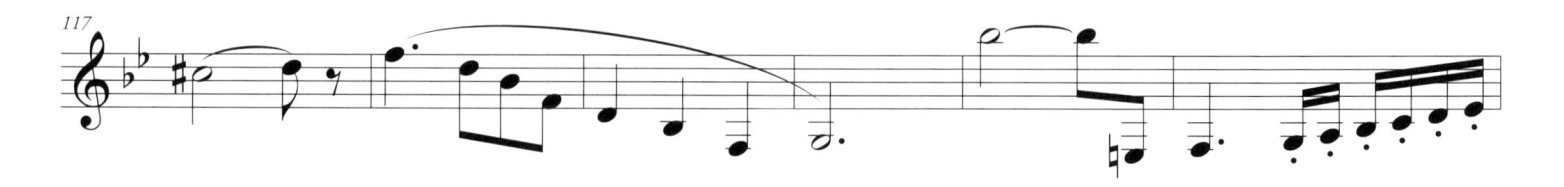

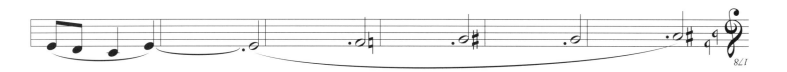

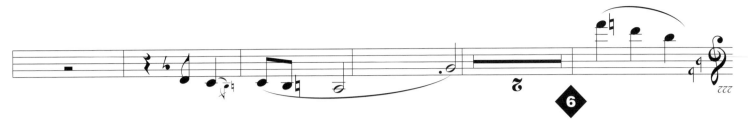

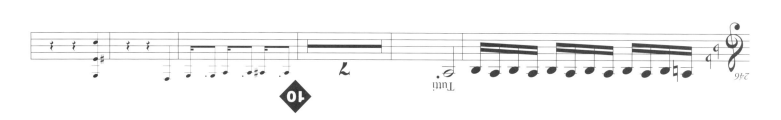

Poco piu animato

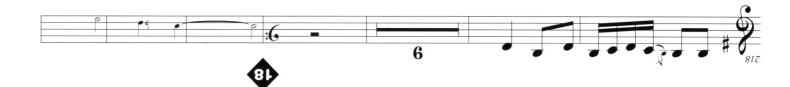

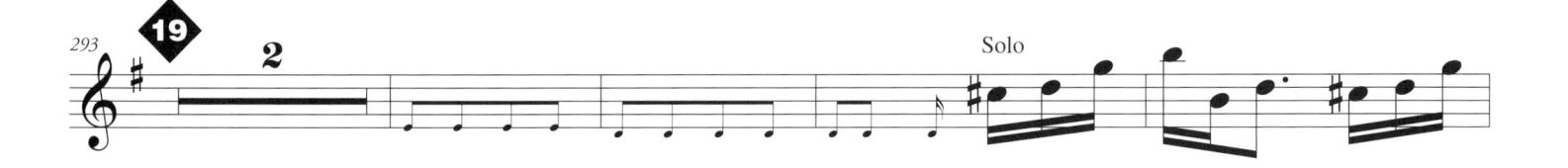

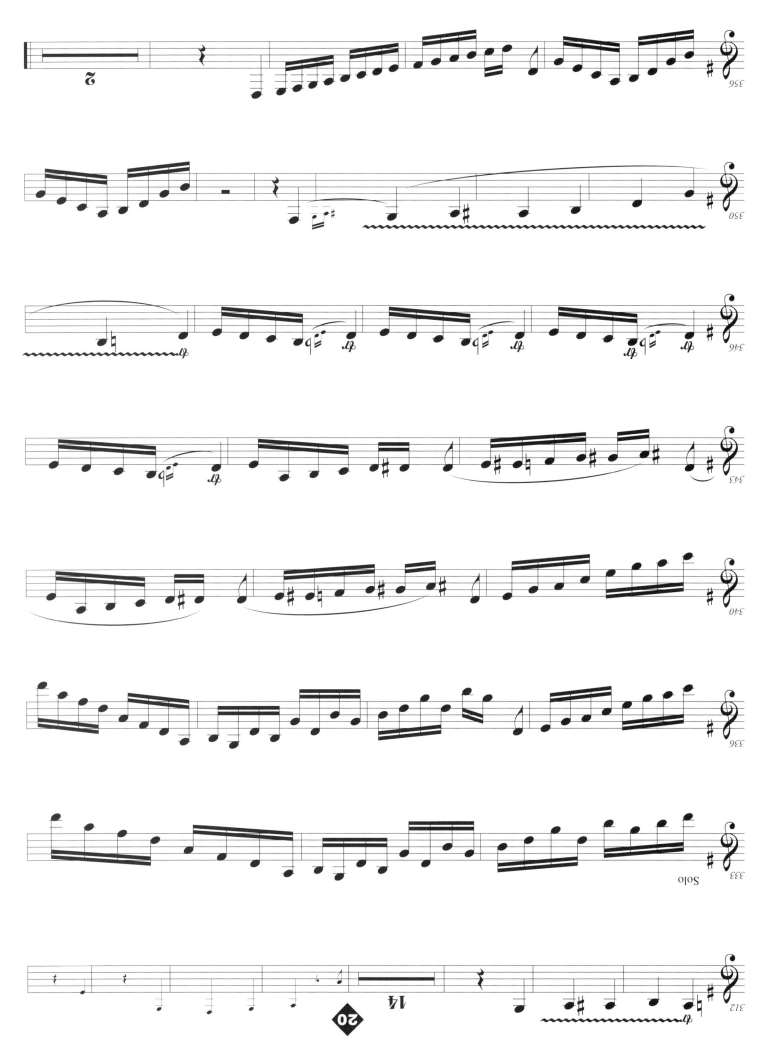